IN THE
WADDISH TIME

IN THE YADDITH TIME

a sonnet sequence

by

Ann K. Schwader

with illustrations

by

Steve Lines

and an introduction

from

Richard L. Tierney

MYTHOS BOOKS, LLC

POPLAR BLUFF

MISSOURI

2007

Mythos Books, LLC
351 Lake Ridge Road
Poplar Bluff
MO 63901
U. S. A.

www.mythosbooks.com

Published by Mythos Books, LLC 2007.

FIRST EDITION

In the Yaddith Time copyright © 2007 by Ann K. Schwader.

Cover art and interior art copyright © 2007 by Steve Lines.

The author asserts her moral right to be identified as the author of this work.

ISBN 13: 978-0-9789911-5-9
ISBN 10: 0-9789911-5-X

Set in *Fusaka* & *Adobe Garamond Pro*.

Fusaka & *Adobe Garamond Pro* by Adobe Systems Incorporated.
www.adobe.com

Typesetting, layout and design by PAW.

For Ben

CONTENTS

ℑℵⱦℜ⊘ⅆ⛊ℭⱦℑ⊘ℵ

In 1926, H.P. Lovecraft wrote what has been called a "sonnet cycle" of thirty-six sonnets embodying a great many of his "eldritch" dreams and visions, some dreamily haunting, some shudderingly ghostly and even ghastly, and a few suggesting the horror of a monstrous, mindless, blind, and purposeless universe—the universe in which we happen to find ourselves living.

Some have speculated that Lovecraft was influenced by the prolific sonneteer Edwin Arlington Robinson, but I suspect that he may also have been inspired by an even darker predecessor, namely the Victorian Age poet James Thomson, author of the long epic poem of darkness and despair, "the City of Dreadful Night." In this gloomy masterpiece, Thomson dwells at length on the indifference of the cosmos, the bleakness and pointlessness of the human condition, and the darkness of mankind's ultimate fate—themes which Lovecraft would later pick up and amplify to an even greater cosmic pitch.

Lovecraft's sonnet cycle "Fungi From Yuggoth" consisted of thirty-six sonnets. The first three began the series as if a narrator were recounting his personal story leading up to his outré dreams and visions, and the rest of the sonnets are evidently the substance of those visionings, the narrative sequence being scrambled or lost altogether.

Now in this slim booklet by Ann Schwader we have the sonnet collection "In the Yaddith Time." It is unabashedly influenced by Lovecraft's sonnet cycle, even to the extent of containing thirty-six sonnets as did his. Moreover, it contains many of the same dark themes. However, rather than being a sonnet "cycle," it is subtitled "A Sonnet Sequence," and this is entirely accurate. For in this case the entire work is a narrative poem from start to finish—an epic of Cthuloid cosmology.

When Ann first sent this work to me I had meant to read it a few sonnets at a time, savoring them, but once I'd started I found I had to keep going until I'd read the whole thing through. The epic narrative nature of the work kept me wanting to find out what happened next. The plot is not complex: Man's first expedition to Mars encounters subterranean horrors akin to Cthulhu and other Old Ones on Earth, the captain of the Earth ship is possessed and forced to voyage with his crew through what seems to be a series of "stargates" to Yuggoth and beyond. From then on the sonnet sequence might well be titled "The Involuntary Hitchhiker's Ride Through the Lovecraftian Cosmos," with stops along the way at Yaddith, the Ghooric Zone, Celaeno, Carcosa, and the Lake of Hali. But this is no bland tourist jaunt, being fraught with terror and madness every warpdrive-hop of the way.

A few of the sonnets have their titles in brackets. These evidently interrupt the flow of the narrative in order to inform the readers of what the Old Ones are up to—how they are influencing the minds of the space travelers in order to bend them to their dark purposes. This strikes me as very much like the explanatory asides written by the ancient Greek playwrights into their tragedies.

The beginning of Schwader's epic reminded me of A.E. Van Vogt's classic tale "The Vault of the Beast," in which an ancient "Great One" imprisoned in a massive tower on Mars is inadvertently almost set free by human explorers. Like Cthulhu on Earth, this being has been trapped in a monstrous tomb-prison on Mars and is now awaiting release by his minions. I strongly suspect Van Vogt was influenced by HPL here.

I greatly enjoyed Schwader's dark tour from Yuggoth through Yaddith, then onward to the Pleiades and the Hyades and finally to the chaotic heat-death of Earth and the Universe. This is Lovecraft's "Fungi From Yuggoth" brought home poetically to watchers of science fiction movies from *Forbidden Planet* all the way up through *Stargate, Sphere, Alien, Andromeda,* and modern cosmology in general.

Unfortunately, only those of us dark acolytes who are steeped in Lovecraftian lore will "get it" when we read this dark epic. Mundane readers should never even attempt it. Not for them are the dark secrets of the cosmos, nor the dark knowledge of impending human destiny.

But those of us who do not shrink from hard truth will recognize that Ann Schwader's cosmic sonnet sequence is nothing less than Lovecraft's "Fungi From Yuggoth" brought up to date in the 21st century.

—Richard L. Tierney

"He had seen Yaddith, yet retained his mind,
And come back safely from the Ghooric zone . . ."

—H. P. Lovecraft,
"Alienation"

⌈ ᛏᚼᚼᛊ
ᛊᛟᚾᏩ ᏌᚼᛁᛏᛁᚾᏩ ⌋

Beyond the pallid sparks of wholesome space,

lost Yaddith drifts forever in her void

of primal nightmare, temple to a race

whose lightest thoughts might leave a world destroyed.

The venom of such dreaming, crystallized,

they wove in matrices to keep it whole

against long journeying—& then devised

an embassy of Wyrms to core the soul

from one ill-omened planet. Drilling deep

in ruddy rock, these minions carved a fane

to guard their charge until the stars again

brought forth their masters' will. Now, coiled in sleep

of centuries, they wait within that gloom

for some faint touch upon the latch of doom.

ᛗ

ナカ丘
〒ェ几ェ几G

T hey waited for us in a cave on Mars,

beneath lost oceans of dread empires past,

within a cavern echoing & vast

as human ignorance. Far stranger stars

than humble Sol had spawned those crystals dark

with bitter prophecy . . . the chill intent

of Powers plotting eons to invent

each facet of damnation. Still, no mark

upon them spoke of danger clear enough

to warn us off; & thus it was we came

like slaughter lambs to marvel at that frame

of twisted yellow metal holding rough-

cut stones in latticework of alien make.

This was our first—& mankind's last—mistake.

ṃ

Ann K. Schwader

THE
RECOGNITION

We ran to fetch our captain left behind

with mechanoids to measure, map, & plot

for colonists to come. Were we so blind?

Cruel hindsight whispers so; but we were not,

except as fate's hand painted us. No sign

of madness marred our leader then: he spoke

of faring outward, nothing more malign—

until that fatal moment when he broke

away alone, too eager for that place.

Though they hung mute before, the crystals rang

to welcome him as though some wind of space

now gusted through their frame . . . & as they sang,

a savage gladness kindled in his eyes.

We fled & left our captain with his prize.

ᛗ

the
first visions

Beneath a moonless sky of molten jet,

amid the jagged fangs of ruined towers,

a robed procession winds . . . with forms not ours,

& lemur eyes of deepest violet . . .

A Singing rises from the very air

(which is not air, nor anything men breathe):

one hundred thousand tongues, so fine & rare

& rich with wisdom . . . *listen, & believe* . . .

So falls the first seed onto fertile soil

long promised to the darkness, & that end

all human striving struggles to pretend

will never come. Beyond such senseless toil,

the Sleepers in their burrows wake at last

to seize this dreaming mind & hold it fast.

THE
FIRST SACRIFICE

We'd barely reached the surface when they came:

quake tremors rippling underfoot like some

great beast aroused from slumber. We froze numb

one fatal moment—then young Waite, whose fame

in xeno-geologic circles made

him curious past caution, turned again

& clambered down that noisome hole. Afraid

for him & for our captain, we rushed then

to rescue both, but found the passage blocked

by freshly tumbled heaps of Martian stone

& Waite crushed dead. Our captain stood alone

clutching that crystal frame. As we gaped, shocked,

he swore the price was cheap for what he'd learned—

& in his eyes, inhuman power burned.

ᛗ

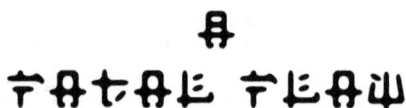

Ann K. Schwader

A
FATAL FLAW

S urely they must have known; the ones who chose

him for command, at least. They ran more tests

than Solomon reborn to find the best

& fittest, soundest, sanest. Madness grows

like any other malady: in genes

these most ingenious fools read like a book

of Holy Writ, & from that scripture took

false comfort in deciding by such means.

They spared no thought for tired antiquities

like Evil, or the doom of Destiny

worked out in willing flesh. Philosophy

& faith alike dismissed, such men as these

perceive the pieces, yet deny the whole—

the subtle poison of a tainted soul.

m

Ann K. Schwader

the
departure

Our captain was the first of us aboard,

    for while we mourned our comrade's death, he sealed

the shuttle's lock behind him—then ignored

our calls for hours. Madness long concealed

soon flowered in the wreckage of our ship's

controls as Engineering, Commo, Nav

became his playthings. Sparking panels ripped

from consoles stole what small chance we might have

of rescue; it appeared beyond all doubt

he'd stranded us. Yet, when confronted, he

denied these dangers. All we needed lay

within that crystal frame we'd found today:

a focal guidepost to infinity . . .

& then the starry dark turned inside out.

♏

⌈ the CALL OF YUGGOTH ⌉

To rend the flimsy veil of space & time

which serves as blindfold to frail mortal brains

too fragile yet for chaos's sublime

& endless vistas . . . to prepare these plains

of frozen methane madness where our Gate

Between the Stars stands ready to admit

such laggard seekers as might stumble late

upon our mysteries . . . thus we submit

ourselves unto our Martian comrades' will.

For Those they serve, we serve: the stars have turned

at last to bring a triumph richly earned.

We *mi-go* wait upon that to instill

the lore of deep Na'morha's ageless heart

in one who comes to tear all things apart.

ᛘ

Ann K. Schwader

☼ ⅄
⅄ꙮ'ꝰꙮⵚⱤⱯꙨ'ⵚ ⱣⱢⱯⵊ⅄

Bone cold in cryskin suits, we stood aghast

at our crazed leader's promised destination—

then searched in vain for any indication

of where he'd landed us. Too dark, too vast

for even Pluto, space curved up & out

in place of sky behind a ragged range

of fractured granite weathered into strange

grim visages. Then came a crewmate's shout:

"The arch!" It rose just as our captain said

we'd find it, starkly alien in form,

& framing stars which seemed abruptly wrong.

Then from those cursed lights flew a buzzing swarm

of half-crustacean Others, clawed & strong . . .

We fought hard, but our chief nav lost her head.

ꝳ

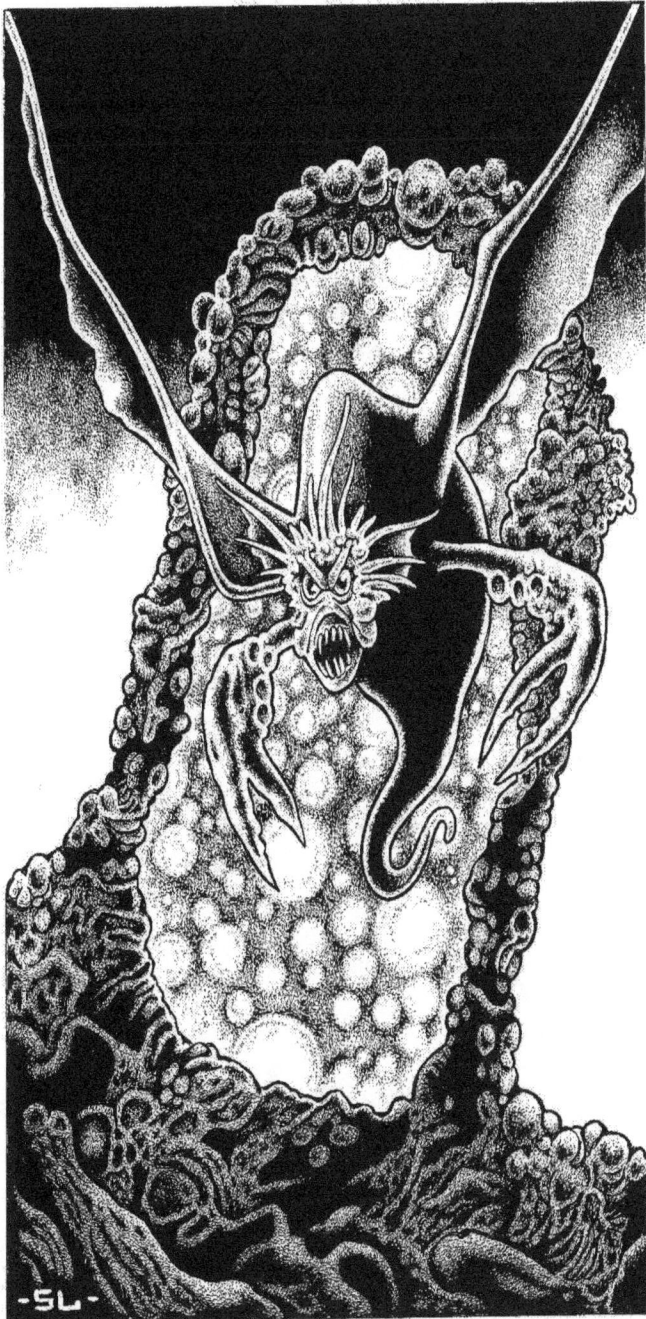

Ann K. Schwader

SACRIFICIAL EYES

Beneath that starry maw, we found a slab

of mottled alien rock, rough trapezoid

with half a hundred stains both bright and drab

from sacrifices past. What hellish void

had claimed our friend, or why, we couldn't guess;

but here her headless body sprawled in gore,

flash-frozen like the rest. There seemed no more

to learn from this fresh tragedy, unless

the answer waited in our own stunned eyes

turned now upon each other—lambs anointed

for ritual destruction. What dark prize

would we be spent for next? Our captain pointed

us towards the chaos framed beyond that stone.

"Through there," he cried, "awaits the Ghooric zone!"

ᛗ

-SL-

Ann K. Schwader

INSIDE
THE GHOORIC ZONE

Black viscous pools within whose fetid deeps

writhed Things our captain knew—but would not name—

assailed our reeling senses. Sentient flame

illuminated temples, fanes, & keeps

where faceless phantoms veiled by yellow silk

penned texts with venomed ink wherein one word

unwisely spoken or by mischance heard

might summon The Unspoken or his ilk.

Thus horror piled on horror till we knew

no law but panic. Mutiny or not,

our nerves urged flight—and flee we did, into

a choking mist of midnight, foul & hot

as devil's breath. Our captain shrieked his hate,

yet he was first to dive back through that gate.

ᛗ

Ann K. Schwader

[IN
NA'MORAH'S HALLS]

Within these green-lit caverns coiling deep,

we trace the twisted ruins of a soul

predestined by our Yaddith lords to reap

forbidden wisdom's whirlwind past control

of mortal flesh & mind. Mere sacrifice

no longer pays the freight of fated change,

yet turns his journey terrible & strange

enough to justify (for us) that price.

Secluded now in our subzero fane,

our task begins anew: to tempt & guide

by slow corruption of one chosen brain,

by crystal oracles mis-clarified,

so that his crew must follow—endlessly—

redshifting phantoms of insanity.

ᛗ

18

⃝⃝⃝⃝⃝⃝⃝
STRANGE STARS

Waking alone, I found the hallways filled

with otherworldly vapors: indigo

shot through by brilliant shafts of sound that shrilled

& rasped along each nerve. What made that glow

(sealed as we were—I thought—in orbit's night)

perturbed my puzzled mind until I sought

our ship's sole viewport cubicle . . . & caught

a glimpse at last of our uncanny plight.

No ordinary void stretched past its pane,

but multi-hued abysses thick with things

which writhed through angled space, or flew on wings

of twisted living fire. I turned again

& stumbled blindly through that bitter door,

realizing we would see our world no more.

ɸ

A DREAM OF AEGYPT

I felt a desert wind sigh through our ship,
spice-scented by that more than ancient East
where gilded Death slinks forth with nightmare's grip
from certain shattered tombs where ghoul packs feast.
Sweet breath of lotus whispered pleasure . . . yet
my flesh recoiled as from a cobra's kiss
& woke me trembling, trying to forget
some lurking half-glimpsed horror in the mists
of my exhausted mind. To clear my head,
I stumbled out—& found the corridor
asquirm with hieroglyphs. Our captain stood
still scrawling with one finger, in fresh blood
I *hoped* was his. Blanching, I asked what for.
"The Messenger awaits," was all he said.

M

Ann K. Schwader

THE
MESSENGER

We rode the shuttle down to what first seemed

a sterile desert world whose suns & sky

& sand all shimmered like some evil dream,

bewildering our irritated eyes

while calling up phantasms from our minds.

The flame-robed cryptic figure who appeared

out of a sudden storm which left us blind

with dust & gasping for our lives was clearly

one of these—until our captain fell

on bended knee before this apparition,

abject as any pilgrim on a mission

to save his soul from ignorance's hell.

"The Messenger?" I queried. *"Yes, the same . . ."*

Our knees all failed us, too, from fear & shame.

m

Ann K. Schwader

Into
the Red Land

How long we wandered on those haunted sands

I never knew for sure, nor risked a guess

at all my surely shattered consciousness

hallucinated there. In taloned hands

more skeleton than flesh, this Messenger

clutched instruments of alien design

& spoke at length of them, both what they were

& how best used (dear God!)—yet still our minds

revolted against knowing what he did.

At last we staggered up one twisted dune

which writhed like some great worm beneath our feet,

& squinting in the twin suns' hellish heat

beheld an ebon structure wrought of runes

& shifting shadows: the Black Pyramid.

m

Ann K. Schwader

THE
WAGES OF PROPHECY

Still following the Messenger, we crept

through passageways within that pyramid

inscribed with imagery which howled & wept

& writhed with some weird history. What did

it mean? We shuddered at our leader's smile

as his sly phantom gestured with a claw

at certain scenes: the violent, the vile.

Writ strange, Earth's chronicle was what we saw.

Past bled into the present, then ran on

down corridors torn deep in living stone,

revealing future horrors still unspawned

which showed mankind had *never* been alone.

A crimson curtain veiled the final plan—

our captain reached to pull it, & we ran.

ᛗ

ナカエ
ＰＲＩＥＣ ＯＴ ＶＩＳＩＯＪ

Both suns were setting as we left that place

of mythic landscapes & lost mysteries

recalling Ægypt's death-cults. Which of these

had made our leader bandage up his face

before rejoining us, we dared not ask.

Whatever auguries he might have viewed,

whatever psychic maelstrom then ensued,

his only presence was a blind white mask.

Some hours later, safe aboard our ship

(oh fond false hope), our medic ventured in

with lasers, sprays, & fresh synthetic skin

to heal the ravages of nightmare's grip.

He left that cabin deathly pale . . . then said

our captain had clawed both eyes from his head.

ᛘ

Ann K. Schwader

A
DREAM OF HOME

I walked on Earth our mother, sweetly green

as legend paints her, clean in sea & sky,

with birdsong in the branches like a cry

of paradise regained . . . until that scene

dream-shifted into chaos. Sudden night

spread shadowwings in one vast inky smear,

erasing daylight as a shriek of fear

arose from every throat: *the stars turn right!*

Mild seas brewed tempests then, & skies split wide,

revealing such uncleanness writhing in

upon our luckless planet from Outside

that men ran mad. Half leaping from my skin

with terror I awoke—to find our crew

all shared my nightmare, screaming it was true.

m

Ann K. Schwader

ᛡᚯᛋᛏ
𐤉ᛉᛡᚠᛡᚼᚯ

Among the clustered sister Pleiades
shines one whose fourth world holds a plundered store
of esoteric wisdom, such weird lore

as gods might whisper—or a madman seize.

The latter led our crew, & so we came

trespassing over centuries of dust

through alien archives bound in gold, or rust,

or crystal . . . or soft skins we feared to name.

Our instruments revealed no other lives

within this labyrinth, & yet it seemed

that shapes slipped past the corners of our eyes.

Too vaporous & faint to analyze,

we knew them still as marvels men once dreamed,

& wondered at the ways that myth survives.

ᛗ

Ann K. Schwader

THE
FATE OF WISDOM

We searched & scavenged hour after hour

down every legend-haunted corridor

of that great library, in quest of power

torn from the lips of wizards at hell's door

on half a thousand worlds. What earthly use

such texts might be to one forever blind,

we could not guess; yet fetched without excuse,

fearing the shadows of our captain's mind.

He crouched outside, a great wyrm on his hoard,

clutching at tablets of cuneiform

he tried to read with fingertips. Ignored,

we added still more findings to that swarm—

then watched it crumble into scraps & clay

as spectral winds blew wisdom's dust away.

ᛗ

Ann K. Schwader

⌈ the WILL OF YADDITH ⌉

As Earth's first masters harnessed shoggoth-kind

to raise aquatic citadels of stone,

compelling by the power of their minds

the transmutation into flesh & bone

of protoplasmic nightmares . . . so We too

compel the onset of unending change

in this our chosen instrument. Deranged

already by his fate, he will not do

as human in the fleeting time remaining.

To sound that final triumph of the void,

to gaze upon all mortal dreams destroyed,

there can be neither flinching nor constraining

the will of Yaddith worked upon this clay

predestined from its birth for blackest days.

 barrel

†ħ£
℈⌇ℛ¥⅚†ǍⱢ ѿ⵿⋂⌐

The crystals had hung silent for so long,

they troubled no one but our engineer

who sometimes—deep in liquor—claimed to hear

their whisperings of some unearthly song

behind his section's door. No breath of air

could breach that hardened bulkhead; yet one night,

we knew that *something* had. Wild peals of fright

& cosmic chaos, madness & despair

rang through the ship until we ran to see

these terrors for ourselves. Our captain swayed

before the alien clamor like a snake

transfixed before its flautist . . . & to make

our fear complete, his supple frame displayed

no hint of bone where human bones should be.

ᛖ

Ann K. Schwader

ᗯᕼᕮᖇᕮ
ᗷᒪᗩᑕK ᔑTᗩᖇᔑ ᖇIᔑᕮ

He claimed his healing lay where black stars rise

at eventide, above a shrouded lake

whose tattered phantoms stalk & cloud-waves break

upon a shore not meant for human eyes

to look upon . . . & ever live content

again. Our captain spoke in riddles now

so frequently we'd ceased to wonder how

these insights came to him, or what he meant

by telling us. Our navigator dead,

we had no means to guess this destination

until we woke to view—just as he'd said—

a planetscape of such unreal sensations,

all logic paled beneath that bleeding sky

whose primary was Taurus's mad eye.

ᛗ

-SL-

Ann K. Schwader

A
DREAM OF SISTERS

We made our camp beside those haunted waters,

our tent domes sealed up tight; & still I dreamed

I wandered in the lake-mists with two daughters

of some lost ancient king. As moonlight gleamed

across their faces veiled by yellow silk,

they murmured of Carcosa & Hali,

Aldones & his foredoomed dynasty.

I comprehended nothing, yet this talk

felt somehow both familiar & malign:

a distant family secret, or a play

half overheard. They spoke as though I, too,

would know my role before this night was through;

& whispered as they faded into day,

"Remember that you bear our father's Sign."

ꝳ

Ann K. Schwader

the
RESTORATION

I woke with trembling fingers clutched around

the oval of some void-dark artifact

which bore a single jaundiced glyph. No sound

escaped my lips, & yet the simple act

of finding this aroused our entire camp

to frantic action. Stumbling from his tent,

our captain caught my hands—his grip as damp

& boneless as a corpse's, with the scent

of burgeoning corruption. Wretched, sick,

I dropped my find & watched him snatch it close,

retreating to that lake where cloud wraiths rose.

We found him later, staring into slick

& viscous waters with *twin pools of black* . . .

Not eyes; not something human looking back.

m

SIGHT
PAST SIGHT

O ur medic vowed that he would understand

not only how, but what those black pits saw;

what made their owner rave & wrench his hands

in arcane gestures. One night, voice rasped raw

with prophecy, our captain spoke out clear:

if any cared to share his sight past sight,

he had a method now to grant them Light.

Our medic raised his hand to volunteer—

just harmless herbs, he claimed, a simple tea

the captain brewed himself, then meditation;

but soon he shrieked of things that Should Not Be,

of watchers in the void, & strange damnations.

These visions ended on a gurgling note.

Next morning, we found out he'd slashed his throat.

m

SOUNDS OF CHANGE

We never saw what tore the cameras down;

but one by one, their bridge screens flickered out.

Our engineer, investigating, found

a dark & nauseous ichor smeared about

the ruins of a dozen. After that,

we took our orders over intercom,

achieving nearly philosophic calm

by means of sedatives. If some great bat

should shriek till panels blew & eardrums burned,

or syllables slurred up from mucous depths,

we hastened to obey our captain's voice

however weirdly varied—for we'd learned

from glimpses too mind-searing to forget

that listening was much the safer choice.

ᛗ

Ann K. Schwader

A
⊄ℝⅇAℳ ⦿ℱ ℙℝ⦿ℙℋⅇℂ¥

I dreamed of waking to a voice I knew:

our navigator's, once; yet sadly changed

since that bleak day when claw-winged Others flew

from Yuggoth's gate & left her . . . *rearranged*,

not dead, she claimed. Half prisoner, half guest,

a disembodied brain within a case

which *mi-go* use for specimens, she'd pressed

beyond all limits of mere time & space

as witness to her captors' chronic thirst

for knowledge, conquest—yes, & exploitation

of countless worlds, our Earth among the worst.

This seemed a hideous incarceration;

yet as I cursed its alien design,

she swore she still preferred her fate to mine.

ⅿ

ᛏᚻᛖ MUTINEERS

They begged me to stand with them. I refused

not out of loyalty, but nameless fear

which worried at our footsteps, & infused

the very air we breathed. Our engineer,

too practical for phantoms, only scoffed.

The captain was incompetent, he said;

they'd seize the ship, & see that madman dead.

I watched his laser carbine, held aloft

like Caesar's eagles, lead them all away . . .

ten breathless minutes later came a roar

like nothing mortal from our captain's door,

then shrieking like a demon-pack at play.

Now I leave ration packets twice a day

for mindless horrors who are men no more.

ᛗ

Ann K. Schwader

MINIONS OF CHAOS

Their rations went unclaimed for several days

before I finally dared investigate

whatever further cruelties ill fate

had dealt my former comrades. Through a maze

of twisted pipes and wiring warped past use,

I traced their faint & maddening refrain:

were these still human voices, though insane,

or mutant prodigies of gene abuse?

At length, a swirling haze of alien tints

sealed off one corridor, as though by force.

Behind it capered parodies of men

who sang & piped & wept . . . then sang again,

until I felt stars faltering off course

with every syllable's soul-withering hints.

m

A
DREAM OF ENTROPY

Alone beyond real sanity, I keep

a weapon close at hand, burn every light

around the clock . . . & struggle not to sleep

till raw exhaustion triumphs over fright,

dragging my ravaged consciousness past night's

event horizon. Silence drains away

into that howling vortex, as both right

& order vanish. One vain speck of clay!

I know myself as merely that—the last

such speck remaining in this ruined shell

adrift between a history now lost

& one not meant for man. It's just as well

I dream so seldom anymore: the veil

of Being wears too thin now, & too frail.

ന

⎡ ¥ＡＤＤエＴＨ'Ｓ ⎤
⎣ ＷエＴＮＥＳＳ ⎦

That fragile candle called the mortal mind

extinguishes so very easily . . .

now only one remains still fit to be

fair witness to our master's last design

unraveling toward its triumphant state

of perfect chaos. Mere flesh cannot bear

such knowledge without damage—thus, we fear

lest stubborn primate ego should abate

her torments prematurely. To protect

this spark until required, we must rely

upon our journey crystals to deflect

self-violence: her brain shall sleep, not die,

within its bone cocoon while time & space

decay at their inexorable pace.

ᛖ

Ann K. Schwader

CONFRONTATION

I woke from dreams that seemed an eon long
to find myself entombed while still alive,

still breathing atmosphere grown foul & strong

with lingering decay. Had I survived

alone, then? Surely not: for through the deck

beneath my feet, a fearful rhythm came,

like some inhuman heart too long shipwrecked

within its corpse. Commingled dread & shame

compelled me to confront the source, & so

I carefully retraced that route I'd vowed

to let alone months . . . *centuries* . . . ago.

Picking my sickened way amid a crowd

of ossified remains, I seized the slide

which sealed our captain's door, & pulled it wide.

⟨ℜℰⱯℰℒ𝔸ℸℐΦℕ⟩

I saw the crystals first; at least, I strove

to focus on them only & ignore

those arabesques of altered flesh which wove

around & through their matrix frame. Yet more

than merely visceral horror fixed my eyes:

old Euclid's theories of geometry

gave way to pan-dimensioned anarchy.

The human mind should not quite realize

what mine did then. All laws of civil space

forsaken with my sanity, I tore

that framework free of what had been a man;

& as I did, our time-worn ship began

fragmenting too. Black chaos surged & roared,

drawing me swiftly toward . . . nowhere. No place.

ⰁⰋ

VOICES
OF YADDITH

No life survives on this burnt bitter rock,

not even mine for long—& yet it seems

that voices whisper in this fading dream

illumined by mortality & shock.

They speak to me of Yaddith First-Created:

a world past ancient, primal whim of One

whose maddened mindless thrashing kindled suns

to be as randomly eliminated

at any future instant. *There.* That spark,

last focus of my failing sight, was ours.

Its feeble death flare flickers & falls dark,

devoured by a thousand nameless powers

rupturing space-time to resume their sway.

The destiny of Man is to give way.

ᛗ

OMENS

Richard Gavin

AVAILABLE TO ORDER

SECRET HOURS

MICHAEL CISCO

AVAILABLE TO ORDER

WALTER C. DEBILL, JR.

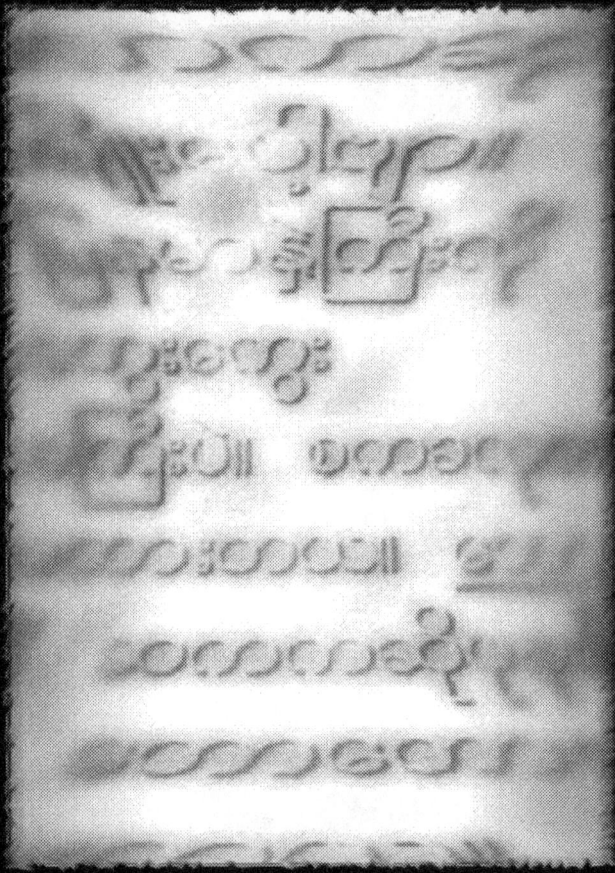

THE BLACK SUTRA

AVAILABLE TO ORDER

UNHOLY DIMENSIONS

JEFFREY THOMAS

AVAILABLE TO ORDER

THE TALES OF INSPECTOR LEGRASSE

H. P. LOVECRAFT & C. J. HENDERSON

AVAILABLE TO ORDER

THE LOVECRAFT CHRONICLES

PETER CANNON

AVAILABLE TO ORDER

www.ingramcontent.com/pod-product-compliance
Lightning Source LLC
Chambersburg PA
CBHW032212040426
42449CB00005B/561